W9-DEU-767

Desert Digits

An Arizona Number Book

Written by Barbara Gowan and Illustrated by Irving Toddy

The author would like to thank Emily Hill of Frontier Elementary School in Payson, Arizona and Samantha Schlatter and Carly and Brianna Fears of Dwight Patterson Elementary School in Mesa, Arizona for suggesting the title of the book.

Sleeping Bear Press™
310 North Main Street, Suite 300
Chelsea, MI 48118
www.sleepingbearpress.com

© 2006 Thomson Gale, a part of the Thomson Corporation.

Thomson, Star Logo and Sleeping Bear Press are trademarks and Gale is a registered trademark used herein under license.

Printed and bound in China.

First Edition

10 9 8 7 6 5 4 3 2 1

Library of Congress Cataloging-in-Publication Data

Gowan, Barbara.
Desert digits : an Arizona number book / written by Barbara Gowan; illustrated by Irving Toddy.
p. cm.
Summary: "This book includes the insects, mountain peaks, saguaro, and more facts all about Arizona. Topics are introduced using numbers and poetry combined with detailed expository text for more in-depth information"—Provided by publisher.
ISBN 1-58536-162-3
1. Arizona—Juvenile literature. 2. Counting—Juvenile literature I. Toddy, Irving.
II. Title.

F811.3G68 2006
979.1—dc22   2006002299

To the three most important people in my life—
my husband, Ed, and our two daughters, Meghan and Kaitlin.

BARBARA

ψ

For my two grandsons,
Azriel Blade Toddy Tsosie and Antonio Guzman.

IRVING

The Gila monster isn't really a monster, but it is the largest (up to 24 inches [61 centimeters] long) and only poisonous lizard native to the United States. Bead-like scales of black and orange, yellow, or pink cover its thick body and short, fat tail.

The mesquite desert scrub is home to the sluggish Gila monster where it spends nearly all of its life underground. During spring, it plods along searching for its favorite foods, quail eggs, and nestlings. This lizard can eat its yearly requirement in several large meals, storing fat in its thick tail. It uses its poison for protection, not for killing prey. Nerve venom drips down the grooved teeth as it bites an attacker. The Gila monster is a food source for hawks, owls, and coyotes.

one

1

1 shy Gila monster
        lives in a burrow under the sand.
    Eating only three meals a year,
            it's the largest lizard in the land.

2 Two-tailed swallowtails
flitter-flutter by,
sipping sweet nectar from the flowers.
It's our state butterfly.

The Two-tailed swallowtail is one of 330 species of butterflies fluttering through Arizona. It can be found soaring through canyons, woodlands, and cities. The long, twin tails protect the butterfly from enemies by attracting attention to its wings instead of its body.

Butterflies have four life stages. Eggs are laid on the host plant, the plant the caterpillar prefers to munch on. The eggs hatch into larvae (tiny caterpillars). Using razor-sharp teeth, the larva devours the leaves, shedding its skin as it grows into a full-sized caterpillar. Finally the caterpillar forms a pupa or chrysalis where its body breaks down and reforms into a winged adult—a butterfly! The butterfly smells with its knobbed antennae and tastes with its legs. It unwinds its proboscis, or coiled feeding straw, to drink.

two

2

3 In the San Francisco Mountains,
peaks reach the sky.
Once an active volcano,
they tower over 12,000 feet high.

Volcanoes in Arizona? Yes!

Visit Flagstaff to see Mount Agassiz, Mount Fremont, and Humphrey's Peak, the highest point in the state. The summit at 12,633 feet (3,851 meters) is above timberline and only alpine plants live in the rocky soil.

The San Francisco Volcanic Field produced more than 600 volcanoes in its six-million-year history. Cinder cones and dark lava flows color the landscape. The San Francisco Peaks volcano erupted over and over from the same vent opening resulting in its magnificent dome shape. These eruptions lasted from 2.8 million to 200,000 years ago. The youngest volcano, nearby Sunset Crater, last erupted in 1065. Geologists say that it is likely that volcano eruptions will occur in Arizona again, although the average time between eruptions is several thousand years.

three

3

4 seasons and 4 directions,
4 sacred mountains stand tall.
4 is a special number
to American Indians, one and all.

All American Indian people refer to the four directions—east, south, west, and north—which play an important role in their traditions and ceremonies. Navajo storytellers talk of four sacred rivers and four sacred mountains when sharing their history. Some stories may take four days to tell. Coyote must swim in the pond four times every morning for four days in the Pima legend. Ceremonies and rituals of spiritual importance are performed in increments of four. A Navajo girl must run every day of her four-day *Kinaaldá*. Major Hopi ceremonies last eight days. The medicine man chants thirty-two songs (a multiple of four) during the Apache Crown Dance ceremony.

four

4

Copper, cattle, cotton, citrus, and climate
are called Arizona's **5** Cs.
Taught to schoolchildren in the state,
they once were the backbone of the economy.

The Five **C**s were a source of many jobs, especially during early statehood years. Copper was king and responsible for the growth of the railroad and numerous Arizona cities. Despite the closure of many mines, Arizona still leads the nation in copper production. Cotton, cattle, and citrus relate to agriculture or farming. Arizona farmers grow enough cotton in a year to make one pair of jeans for nearly every person in the United States. Cattle ranchers produce enough beef for every Arizonan to have a quarter-pound (0.11-kilogram) burger 300 days a year. The citrus crop yields tons of lemons, grapefruit, tangerines, and oranges. The mild, sunny climate attracts tourists. A new, sixth C, computers and high tech industry, employ many Arizonans in the new millennium.

five

5

Zip, buzz, back flip, glisten and whirl,
dart, dive, hover, zoom and zing—
6 tiny hummingbirds
flash their colorful wings.

A hummingbird is an amazing animal. It can reach speeds of 60 miles (96.6 kilometers) per hour in a dive display or appear to hover motionless as it slurps nectar from trumpet-shaped flowers with its long, bristle-tipped tongue. Sweet nectar is an excellent energy food and insects and spiders provide needed protein and fat. The oversized heart beats up to 1,200 times in a minute pumping fuel and oxygen to flight muscles. According to ornithologist Crawford Greenewalt, if a man used energy at a hummingbird's rate, he would need to eat more than a thousand quarter-pound hamburgers in a day!

Ramsey Canyon, a Nature Conservancy preserve in the Huachuca Mountains, is a hummingbird hotspot. Situated at a crossroads of two deserts and two mountain ranges, it serves as a corridor for migrating birds. Fourteen species of hummers have been recorded here.

six

6

7 nuggets of gold
shine in the prospector's pan.
"Eureka!" he shouts.
"I'll soon be a rich man!"

Gold fever hit Arizona in 1858 when Jake Snively swished a pan through the Gila River and the heavy gold flakes settled to the bottom. Gold seekers hit pay dirt in 1863. Prospectors armed with their buckets, shovels, and pans stood in icy water, enduring aching backs, sore knees, and numb feet for a chance at finding gold. Lynx Creek, near Prescott, yielded more than two million dollars' worth of gold, the largest amount of any streamed in the state. It is still a favorite spot for prospecting.

Mountain man Pauline Weaver led an expedition through dangerous Apache territory. The lucky prospectors found nuggets scattered atop a mountain they later named Rich Hill. Nearby, Henry Wickenburg discovered the Vulture mine, the richest ore deposit in the state. Gold can be found in all Arizona counties.

seven

7

Sensory hairs on its **8** legs
help the scorpion locate its dinner.
It can kill its prey immediately
with its pincers and poison-filled stinger.

Two–four–six–eight legs (or four pairs) identify the scorpion as a member of the Arachnid class and cousin to spiders. The 5-inch (12.7-centimeter) long giant hairy scorpion is the largest scorpion in the U.S. and one of 43 species found in Arizona. Scorpions are poisonous. Feeding at night, a scorpion uses a pair of crab-like pincers to capture its prey, usually large insects, centipedes, and spiders. At the end of its long, curved tail is a sharp, hollow stinger that injects the deadly nerve venom. Scorpions inhabit dark, damp places, often hiding in cracks. Children may develop severe symptoms if stung. Take precautions. Wear shoes outdoors, especially around the pool at night. Do not leave shoes, clothing, or towels outside. Look before you place your hand under or into something. Prevention is the best medicine!

eight
8

Good news! Twenty-eight species of bats can be found in Arizona. Bats are important to our ecology. A single bat can consume up to 600 mosquitoes in one hour while a large colony can eat up to 500,000 pounds (226,800 kilograms) of insects, centipedes, and scorpions every night. The Mexican long-tongued bat and the lesser long-nosed bat feed only on the nectar and pollen of night-blooming flowers like the agave and the saguaro cactus. The bat burrows into the flower and uses its long, slender, brush-tipped tongue to lap up nectar. It gets dusted with pollen, which it then transfers to the next flower it visits, aiding in pollination. If disturbed by humans, roosting bats will abandon their young. Please help protect our Arizona bats.

nine

9

Sweet saguaro blossoms
colored creamy white
attract 9 hungry bats
flying in the night.

Named for the muddy, red sediments carried in its water, the Colorado River begins its journey high in the Rocky Mountains and flows 1,450 miles (2,333 kilometers) to the Gulf of California. Through northern Arizona, the Colorado River carved out a great gorge, 277 miles (446 kilometers) long, known as the Grand Canyon. Over time, the raging river filled with sand, and boulders eroded or wore away at the solid layers of rock underneath, creating a channel. Today this canyon is over 1 mile (1.6 kilometers) deep and 10 miles (16 kilometers) wide. Weather and water erosion continue to carve the canyon. The average depth of the Colorado River within Grand Canyon National Park is 40 feet (12.2 meters). Adventure seekers enjoy the white-water rapids, cascading waterfalls, and calm pools as they run the Colorado River in their kayaks and rubber rafts.

ten
10

Splashing down the Colorado River
are **10** rafters, strong and brave,
through white water and whirlpools,
rapids, canyons, and caves.

11 jackrabbits,
      hares with large hind feet,
  move their long ears to catch sounds,
        and when distressed thump their feet.

Did you know that the jackrabbit's long, paper-thin ears act as a cooling system? Blood vessels in the ears are located just under the skin. As the air flows around the ears, it cools the blood. The jackrabbit has special adaptations for desert life. Jackrabbits do not need to drink water because they get sufficient moisture from the green plants they eat. When frightened, the jack can leap up to 20 feet (6 meters) and achieve speeds of 40 miles (76.4 kilometers) per hour. It will flash the white underside of its black tail to alert other jacks and to confuse its predators—the coyote, bobcat, and fox. In the evening, adult jackrabbits often gather together. The black-tailed jackrabbit and the antelope jackrabbit are just two of the 135 species of mammals that live in Arizona.

eleven
11

12 hikers pitch their tents
beneath the rocky ledge,
clinging close to the canyon wall
far away from the edge.

There are thousands of canyons in Arizona, from the immense Grand Canyon over 10 miles (16 kilometers) across to narrow slot canyons barely wide enough for one person to squeeze through. A canyon has steep walls resulting from water eroding, or cutting through, the rock layers over a very long time, often millions of years. In the center of the state near Sedona is Oak Creek Canyon, a favorite spot for hikers. Red rock cliffs tower above and trails wind through oak forests, across the creek, and up the canyon. Water from snowmelt flows through the canyon in spring. During summer hikers cool off by shooting down the slippery rocks at Slide Rock State Park. Colorful autumn leaves followed by winter snow make Oak Creek Canyon a beautiful spot to hike year-round.

twelve
12

Arizona's long journey to statehood began in 1848 as the war with Mexico ended. Land north of the Gila River was given to the United States. Several years later the Gadsden Purchase added the remainder of the land that would become Arizona. In 1863 President Lincoln signed the bill to make Arizona a territory and the capital was established in Prescott in 1864. Territorial governors and officials would try for nearly fifty years to get a statehood bill approved. To demonstrate that Arizona was ready to become a state, the Capitol building in Phoenix was constructed in 1901. Finally on February 14, 1912, President Taft signed the bill making Arizona a state, the 48th to join the Union. George W. P. Hunt was inaugurated as the first state governor.

thirteen
13

Our state flag flies high
over the Capitol every day—
a copper star and field of blue
with **13** red and yellow rays.

Barrel racing is the only rodeo event that cowgirls can participate in. It takes a talented horse and expert rider to weave in and around the barrel course at lightning speed. Steer wrestling lasts only a few seconds. The cowboy rides up beside the running steer, leaps off his horse, and grabs and twists the animal's horns forcing the huge steer to fall flat. Bull riding is considered the most dangerous event as a contestant rides bareback on a raging, kicking bull for eight seconds. If he falls off, a rodeo clown runs out to distract the bull allowing the rider to run to safety. Bronco riding evolved from the task of training wild, untamed horses or broncos to work the cattle ranches. Calf roping showcases the ranch hand's skills needed during the roundup on the range.

Rodeos are popular throughout the state, especially in Payson and Prescott, cities that have hosted rodeos since the 1880s.

fourteen

14

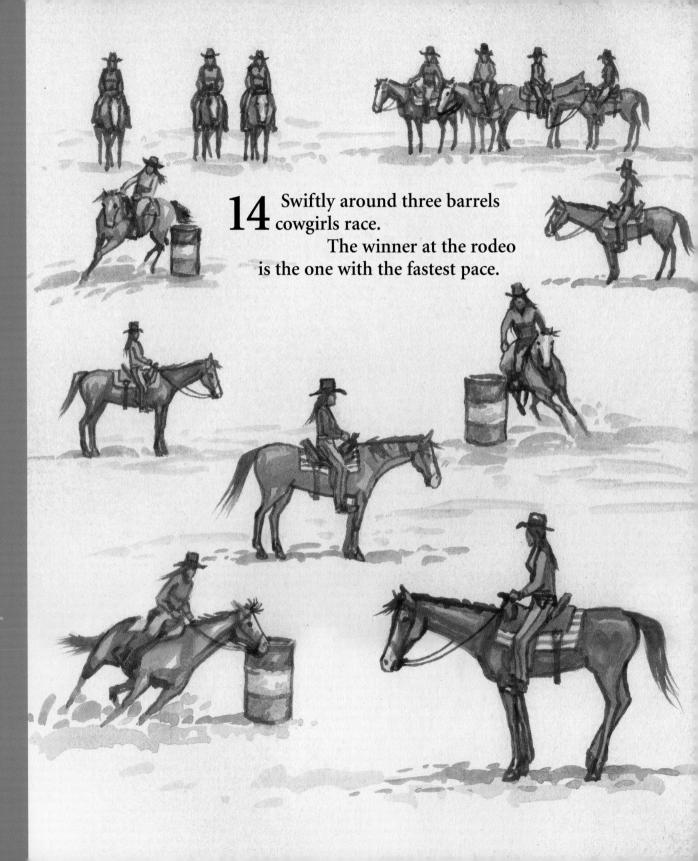

14 Swiftly around three barrels cowgirls race.
The winner at the rodeo is the one with the fastest pace.

Pincushion, hedgehog, organ pipe,
and 15 kinds of prickly pear—
desert cacti with odd names,
even a cholla called teddy bear.

Arizona is the only state where four deserts are found—the Great Basin, Chihuahuan, Mojave, and Sonoran. Lack of water affects the plants and animals that live in the desert ecosystem. The cactus family flourishes in the desert. Most cacti are succulents. Shallow roots absorb water from a rainstorm and transport it to its thick, fleshy, wax-coated stems for storage. Most cacti do not have leaves. Prickly spines protect the plant from sunburn and trap warm insulating air on freezing nights.

Cacti range in size from the half-inch (1.3-centimeter) pincushion to the 65-foot (19.8 meter) giant saguaro. A prickly pear is identified by its pancake-shaped, flat pads, while a cholla [CHO-ya] is made up of sausage-shaped segments. The teddy bear cholla looks like it's coated in soft fuzz, but a closer examination reveals sharp spines. Ouch!

fifteen
15

The "Main Street of America," Route 66, stretched nearly 2,500 miles (4,023 kilometers) from Chicago to Los Angeles. Across Arizona it followed the path of ancient Indians, Spanish conquistadors, and the transcontinental railroad. It became the main street through towns like Holbrook, Flagstaff, and Oatman. It was completed in 1932; devastated farm families trying to escape the drought drove it westward to California and new opportunities. During World War II, men traveled along Route 66 to their military training bases in the West. Postwar cross-country motorists sought adventure on the "Mother Road." By 1970 nearly all of Route 66 was replaced by a fast, modern freeway. The longest remaining leg of this historic highway is a 90-mile (145-kilometer) stretch between Seligman and Kingman, Arizona.

twenty

20

Gas was **20** cents a gallon
driving from Chicago to L.A.
on Route 66,
America's most famous highway.

Forests cover approximately 25 percent of Arizona land. The ponderosa pine forest, the largest in the world, blankets the Colorado Plateau. Trees can reach over 150 feet (46 meters) tall and 4 feet (1.2 meters) across and can live over 300 years. At seven years of age, the pine begins to produce large, egg-shaped cones holding thirty to seventy seeds. Winged seeds take two years to mature and float to the ground when the cone opens in the fall.

Over 1,000 species of plants and animals are closely associated with the ponderosa pine forest. The Abert's squirrel depends so completely on the pine for its survival that it is found only in these forests. This bushy-tailed, tassel-eared squirrel feeds on pinecone seeds, tree buds, and the sugary inner bark of the twigs. Basketball-size nests of twigs and cones are built high in the branches.

30 seeds are safely hidden
tucked inside the pinecone
until fall when the cone opens
and the seeds become windblown.

40 tasty tortillas
start as a soft dough ball.
Pat and roll to flatten,
then cook on a hot comal.

Do you like to eat Mexican food? If you do, then you must like tortillas. Tortillas are thin, flat bread made from wheat flour or corn *masa*. It is baked on a *comal*, a heavy, round griddle. Cowboys use tortillas filled with meat as a convenient way to eat around the campfire. Then, they don't need silverware! Tortillas can be eaten for breakfast, lunch, or dinner. They are used to make tacos, tostadas, burritos, enchiladas, and quesadillas. A favorite way to eat them is warm, right off the comal, with a dab of butter, or *mantequilla*.

forty
40

Kartchner Caverns State Park in the Whetstone Mountains of southeastern Arizona is a masterpiece of nature. For hundreds of thousands of years, water has seeped through the limestone mountain dissolving the rock, carving out a huge cavern, and creating magnificent *speleothems*, or cave decorations. Water droplets dripping from the cave ceiling create a long, thin, hollow tube of calcite growing approximately 1 inch (2.5 centimeters) every 750 years. A soda straw stalactite hanging in Kartchner Caverns is over 21 feet (6.4 meters) long! Water splashing on the floor solidifies into mounds of crystal stalagmites. A 58-foot (17.7-meter) high column adorns the Throne Room. Inside this "living" cave, speleothems continue to form. Visitors entering the cave must be careful not to damage this fragile ecosystem. Kartchner Caverns has been named one of the ten most beautiful caves in the world.

In Kartchner Caverns **50** stalactites grow
as the water slowly drips.
Hanging from the cave ceiling,
one measures over 20 feet from top to tip!

Chipped into the rock
and painted on the cliffs
telling ancient stories
are **60** petroglyphs.

Wherever prehistoric people lived in the Southwest, you will find rock art. Petroglyphs are pictures of plants, animals, humans, or geometric designs that were pecked or carved using a stone tool into a dark rock. Petroglyphs are easily viewed at Newspaper Rock in the Petrified Forest National Park and the Deer Valley Rock Art Center in Phoenix. Figures painted on sheltered rock walls are called pictographs. In Canyon de Chelly (da-shay) National Monument, the Anasazi people painted symbols on the wall above a cliff house over 1,000 years ago. A Navajo pictograph tells the story of a Spanish military expedition with riders wearing heavy cloaks and carrying muskets. Archeologists study rock art to learn how the early people lived.

The American Indians of the Southwest are skilled artists known for creating woven baskets, painted pottery, colorful rugs, and beautiful jewelry. The Navajo learned the skill of the silversmith from the Mexicans over a century ago. Early Navajo jewelers melted coins to obtain silver and added polished turquoise nuggets to their squash blossom necklaces and concho belts. Navajo people believe that wearing turquoise brings good fortune. You can buy jewelry created by modern Indian artists at the Heard Museum Indian Fair and Market in Phoenix, or the Hubbell Trading Post on the Navajo reservation near Ganado.

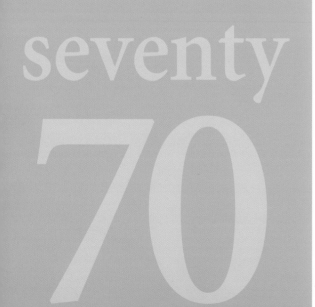

Beads of shell, discs of silver,
and chunks of turquoise   **70** pieces of jewelry
are crafted into
worn by Indian girls and boys.

80 Houseboats, sailboats, and ski boats—
boats in all.
Let's have fun at Lake Havasu
winter, spring, summer, and fall.

eighty
80

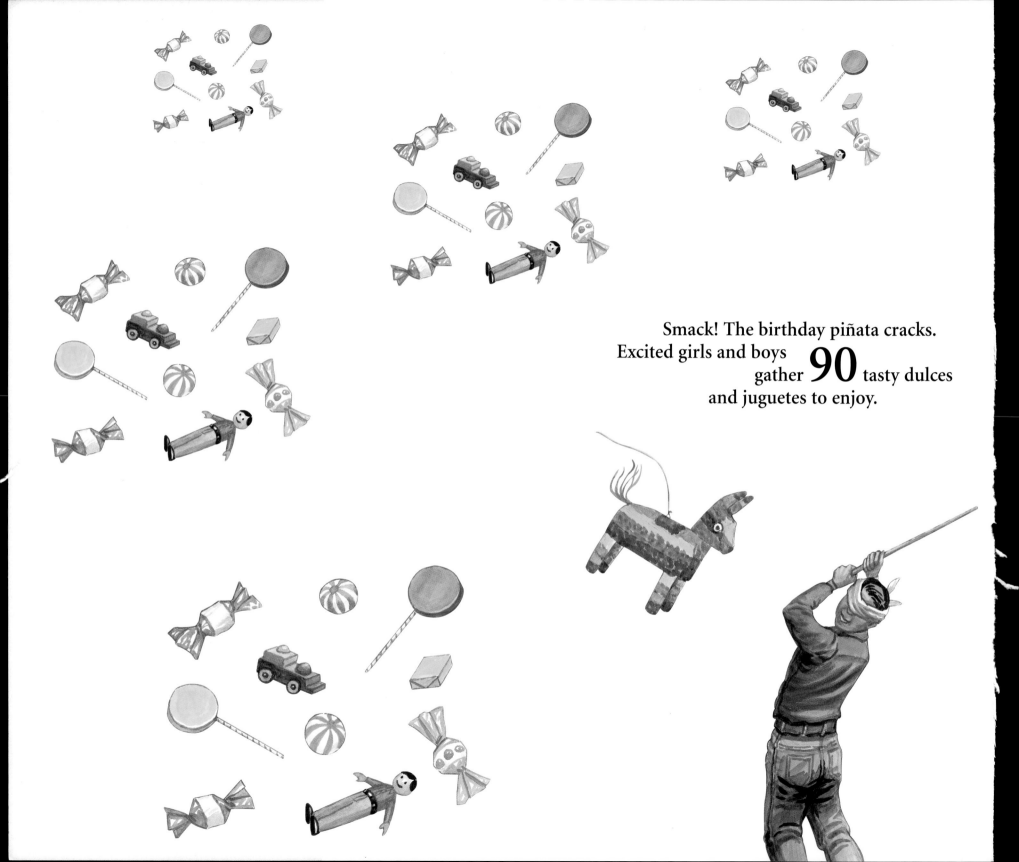

Smack! The birthday piñata cracks.
Excited girls and boys
        gather **90** tasty dulces
and juguetes to enjoy.

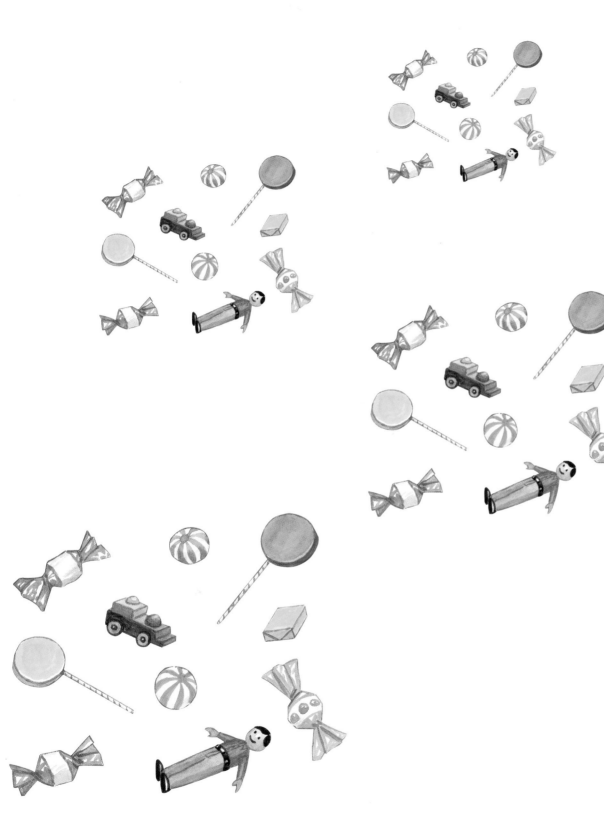

Breaking the piñata is a favorite party game at children's birthday celebrations. The piñata made of papier-mâché and decorated with brightly colored tissue and crepe paper is filled with *dulces* (candy) and *juguetes* (toys). Children form a circle around the suspended piñata and take turns trying to break it open with a *palo* or bat. Usually the child is blindfolded, twirled around and given three chances to bash the piñata. When successful, everyone scrambles to grab his or her share of the treats.

The origin of the piñata dates back to the thirteenth century in China where it was used to celebrate the coming of spring. The explorer Marco Polo introduced it to Europe and the Spaniards brought the custom to Mexico where it became part of the Christmas celebration. Today, piñatas are used around the world to celebrate special occasions.

ninety
90

There are three climate zones in the state: the low desert, the high desert and foothills, and the mountains. The low desert has average high Fahrenheit temperatures in the 60s (around 20 degrees Celsius) in January to over 100 degrees Fahrenheit (38 degrees Celsius) in July. Rainfall is less than 10 inches (25.5 centimeters) a year with most of it occurring in winter and late summer. As the land elevation increases, the temperature decreases and there is more precipitation. Weather is cooler and wetter in the mountains. Summertime high Fahrenheit temperatures are in the upper 70s (around 26 degrees Celsius). The record cold temperature in Arizona was −40 degrees Fahrenheit (-40 degrees Celsius) at Hawley Lake in the White Mountains. A winter storm in Flagstaff dumped 86 inches (218.5 centimeters) of snow in nine days. Throughout the state, humidity is usually very low and the sun shines over 300 days a year.

one
hundred
100

Float in the river
beneath the tall trees
when the temperature soars
to **100** degrees.

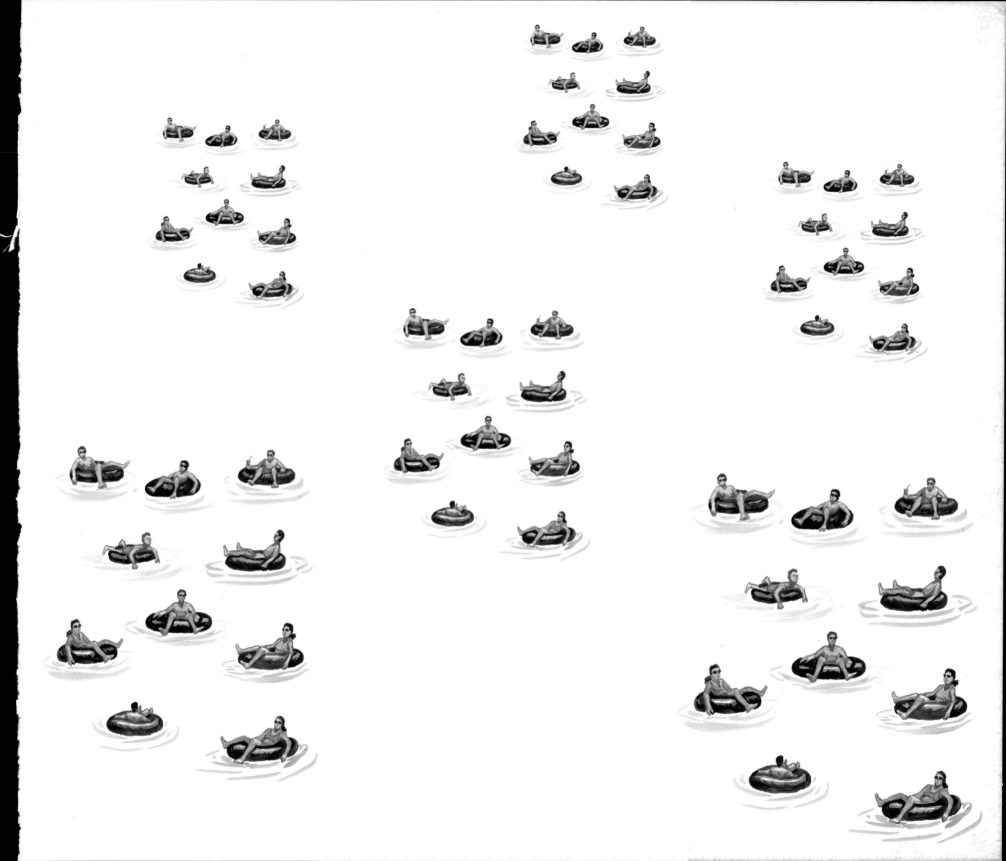

Glossary

alpine plants: living above the timberline

calcite: a common mineral made up of calcium carbonate crystals

cinder cones: small volcanoes shaped like a cone (round base tapering to a point) that form by the accumulation of ash and cinders

Colorado plateau: high country with level terrain cut by deep canyons, found in northeastern Arizona

conquistador: a conqueror from Spain

corridor: passageway

drought: a shortage of rainfall over a period of time

economy: the system of producing, distributing, and consuming goods and services

ecosystem: a community of plants, animals, soil, and climate that interact with each other

elevation: height of land above sea level

erosion: the wearing away of the land by water, wind, and ice

expedition: journey

geologist: a scientist who specializes in the study of the Earth's crust and its layers

high tech industries: businesses dealing with the use of advanced equipment in the fields of electronics, engineering, and computers

Kinaaldá: the traditional coming-of-age ceremony for Navajo girls

mesquite: a desert tree belonging to the pea family

millennium: a period of a thousand years

nerve venom: a poisonous fluid that affects the specialized cells that conduct messages throughout the body

ornithologist: a scientist who specializes in the study of birds

pay dirt: soil containing mineral ore found by a prospector

pollination: transfer of pollen grains to the stigma of the flower so that a seed can form

precautions: actions taken to ward off danger

precipitation: rain, snow, hail, mist, or sleet that falls to the ground

predator: an animal that hunts and kills other animals for food

prey: an animal that is hunted or killed for food by other animals

refuges: protected areas

sediment: small particles that are heavier than water, like mud, sand, or silt

species: a group of animals or plants that have the same characteristics

stalactite: a rock deposit resembling an icicle that is formed by dripping water from the roof of a limestone cave

succulents: plants that store water in their fleshy leaves and stems

territory: an area of land that does not have the full authority of statehood